Oxford Read and Di

C000130867

Life i
Rainforests

Cheryl Palin

Contents

OXFORD
UNIVERSITY PRESS

OXFORD

UNIVERSITY PRESS

Great Clarendon Street, Oxford OX2 6DP

Oxford University Press is a department of the University of Oxford. It furthers the University's objective of excellence in research, scholarship, and education by publishing worldwide in

Oxford New York

Auckland Cape Town Dar es Salaam Hong Kong Karachi Kuala Lumpur Madrid Melbourne Mexico City Nairobi New Delhi Shanghai Taipei Toronto

With offices in

Argentina Austria Brazil Chile Czech Republic France Greece Guatemala Hungary Italy Japan Poland Portugal Singapore South Korea Switzerland Thailand Turkey Ukraine Vietnam

OXFORD and OXFORD ENGLISH are registered trade marks of Oxford University Press in the UK and in certain other countries

© Oxford University Press 2010

The moral rights of the author have been asserted

Database right Oxford University Press (maker)

First published 2010
2021
20

No unauthorized photocopying

All rights reserved. No part of this publication may be reproduced, stored in a retrieval system, or transmitted, in any form or by any means, without the prior permission in writing of Oxford University Press, or as expressly permitted by law, or under terms agreed with the appropriate reprographics rights organization. Enquiries concerning reproduction outside the scope of the above should be sent to the ELT Rights Department, Oxford University Press, at the address above

You must not circulate this book in any other binding or cover and you must impose this same condition on any acquirer

Any websites referred to in this publication are in the public domain and their addresses are provided by Oxford University Press for information only. Oxford University Press disclaims any responsibility for the content

ISBN: 978 0 19 464380 1

An Audio Pack containing this book and an Audio download is also available, ISBN 978 0 19 402183 8

This book is also available as an e-Book, ISBN 978 0 19 464723 6.

An accompanying Activity Book is also available, ISBN 978 0 19 464390 0

Printed in China

This book is printed on paper from certified and well-managed sources.

ACKNOWLEDGEMENTS
Illustrations by: Martin Bustamante/Advocate Art p.6; Fiammetta Dogi/The Art Agency p.14; Kelly Kennedy pp.9, 17, 21; Alan Rowe pp.27, 28, 32, 34, 38, 40, 45, 46, 47; Mark Ruffle pp.4, 26.

The publisher would like to thank the following for their kind permission to reproduce photographs and other copyright material: Alamy Images pp.11 (Piranha/Redmond Durrell), 16 (Hoatzins/Kuttig - Travel), 17 (Cassowary/Holger Ehlers), 19 (Penan tribesman/Nigel Hicks), 20 (cattle/Evan Bowen-Jones); Ardea pp.3 (Brown-throated Three-toed Sloth/M. Watson), 3 (tarantula/Nick Gordon), 12 (Brown-throated Three-toed Sloth/M. Watson), 13 (duck-billed platypus/D.Parer & E.Parer-Cook), 15 (tarantula/Nick Gordon); Corbis pp.21 (burned rainforest/Gustavo Gilabert); FLPA pp.11 (yellow anaconda/Jurgen & Christine Sohns), 14 (orchid mantis/Thomas Marent/Minden Pictures), 16 (Australian King Parrot/Thomas Marent/Minden Pictures), 23 (splendid leaf frog/Piotr Naskrecki/Minden Pictures), 36 (Australian King Parrot/Thomas Marent/Minden Pictures); Nature Picture Library pp.3 (hummingbird/Nick Garbutt), 9 (Sumatran Orang utan/Anup Shah), 17 (hummingbird/Nick Garbutt); NHPA p.15 (Borneo Rhinoceros beetle/Andrea Ferrari); Photolibrary pp.3 (Kapok tree/Stefan Huwiler/imagebroker.net), 7 (Kapok tree/Stefan Huwiler/imagebroker.net), 8 (rubber tapper/Bjorn Svensson/age fotostock), 10 (Amazon river/White), 13 (platypus/Ingo Schulz/imagebroker.net), 22 (tiger/Juniors Bildarchiv); Survival International pp.18 (Penan children building a hut/© Nick and Andy Rain), 19 (Penan people making sago flour/© Nick and Andy Rain).

The charitable organization Survival International helps tribal peoples defend their lives, protect their lands and determine their own futures. http://www.survivalinternational.org

With thanks to Ann Fullick for science checking

Introduction

A tropical rainforest is a forest of tall trees that's warm all year. It's called a rainforest because it usually rains every day. It can rain more than 250 centimeters in one year. Many amazing animals and plants live in rainforests.

tarantula

sloth

kapok tree

hummingbird

What do you know about tropical rainforests?
How tall is a kapok tree?
How long does a sloth sleep every day?
How many eyes does a tarantula have?
What do hummingbirds drink?

Discover!

Now read and discover more about life in tropical rainforests!

Tropical Rainforests

All the tropical rainforests are near the equator. Most of them are in the Tropics. The biggest tropical rainforest is the Amazon rainforest in South America. The second biggest is the Congo rainforest in Africa. South Asia also has lots of tropical rainforests. There are smaller rainforests in Central America, Madagascar, India, Australia, and on the islands near Australia.

Tropical Rainforests on Earth

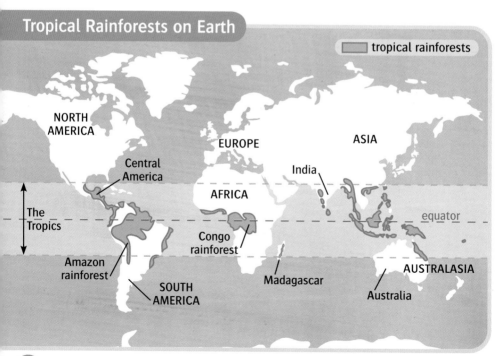

tropical rainforests

NORTH AMERICA

EUROPE

ASIA

Central America

India

AFRICA

The Tropics

equator

Amazon rainforest

Congo rainforest

Madagascar

AUSTRALASIA

SOUTH AMERICA

Australia

Tropical rainforests cover only about 6 percent (%) of Earth, but they have 50% of all the different types of animal and plant that we know. About 10 square kilometers of rainforest can have 750 types of tree, 1,500 types of other plant, 400 types of bird, and 150 types of butterfly.

Some very big animals live in tropical rainforests. Jaguars are the biggest cats in the Amazon rainforest.

A Jaguar

Go to pages 24–25 for activities.

Rainforest Layers

eagle

leaves

bat

emergent layer

branch

monkey

canopy

toucan

jaguar

tree frog

understory

anteater

roots

forest floor

Tropical rainforests have layers. The top layer is the emergent layer. The tops of the tallest trees are in this layer. It's very windy! Eagles and bats live here.

The next layer is the canopy. The big branches and leaves of the tall trees are here. There are many types of animal in this layer, because there's light and lots of food. Monkeys and toucans live in the canopy.

The next layer is the understory. The tops of the small trees are in this layer. It's dark and hot. Jaguars and tree frogs live here.

The bottom layer is the forest floor. The roots of the trees are in this layer. Many insects live on the forest floor. Some big animals like anteaters live here, too. They eat the insects.

A Kapok Tree

Discover!
The kapok tree is one of the tallest rainforest trees. It can grow up to 70 meters tall.

Go to pages 26–27 for activities.

Plants

Animals and people get lots of food from rainforest plants. Bananas, pineapples, and nuts all grow in the rainforest.

We can make things from rainforest plants, too. People make clothes and bags from pineapple leaves. We also use some plants to make medicines. We can use some rainforest trees, like the balsa tree, for wood. We can use the rubber tree for latex to make rubber.

Getting Latex from a Rubber Tree

latex

Orang-Utans in a Nest

Many rainforest plants are homes for animals, like monkeys, birds, and insects. Some frogs sleep between the leaves of big plants. Some birds and other small animals live in tree holes. They make nests for their babies in the holes. Orang-utans sleep in nests in trees. They make the nests from leaves and branches.

Discover!

Orang-utans use big leaves as umbrellas when it rains!

→ Go to pages 28–29 for activities.

The Amazon River

Tropical rainforests have some of the biggest rivers on Earth, like the Mekong River in Asia and the Congo River in Africa. The biggest rainforest river is the Amazon River in South America. The Amazon is about 6,400 kilometers long.

Many smaller rivers go into big rainforest rivers. More than 1,000 smaller rivers go into the Amazon.

A Piranha

An Anaconda

Many animals live in rainforest rivers. The Amazon has more than 3,000 types of fish. One example is the piranha. It has big teeth. Anacondas also live here. The anaconda is one of the biggest snakes in the world.

People need rainforest rivers, too. Rivers give people fish to eat, and water. Rivers are also important for travel. Many people travel by boat because there aren't many roads.

Go to pages 30–31 for activities.

Mammals

A mammal is an animal that breathes air and drinks milk from its mother. Lots of mammals live in rainforests. Chimpanzees are mammals, and they live in African rainforests. They eat leaves, fruit, insects, and other small animals.

Sloths live in the rainforests in Central America and South America. They are the slowest mammals in the world. They eat leaves and fruit, and they sleep for about 18 hours every day!

A Sloth

Discover!

Sloths are so slow that algae grow on their fur!

fur

algae

Tigers live in rainforests in Asia. They are the biggest cats in the world. They hunt and eat other big mammals, fish, and birds. They like water and they can swim well.

Platypuses live in rainforests in Australia. They hunt underwater and they eat insects, shellfish, and worms. Male platypuses have poisonous stingers on their feet.

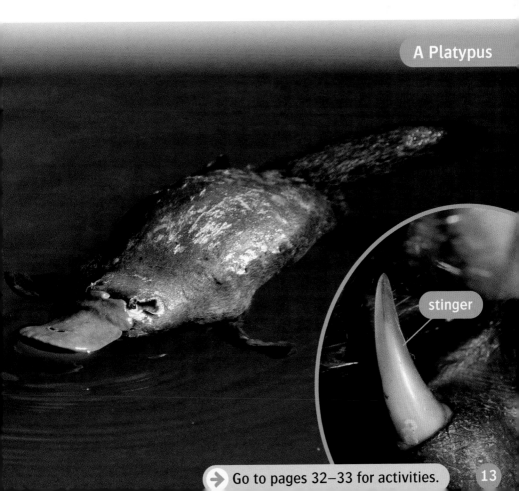

A Platypus

stinger

Go to pages 32–33 for activities.

Minibeasts

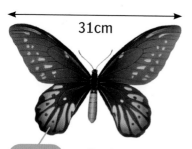

31cm

wing

Most of the minibeasts in rainforests are insects. The biggest butterfly in the world lives in the rainforest in Papua New Guinea near Australia. It's the female Queen Alexandra's Birdwing. Its wings can be 31 centimeters across.

Mantises live in rainforests all around the world. They use camouflage to hide from other animals. They can look like leaves, sticks, or flowers!

A Flower Mantis

horn

A Rhinoceros Beetle

Many types of beetle live in the rainforest. Rhinoceros beetles have a horn on their head like rhinos. They are big and strong.

Spiders live in rainforests, too. Tarantulas live in South American rainforests. They are probably the biggest spiders in the world. Their legs can be 30 centimeters long.

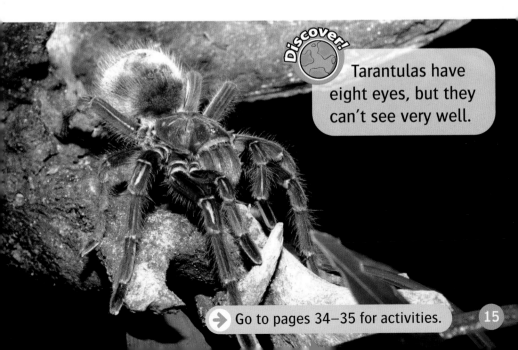

Discover!

Tarantulas have eight eyes, but they can't see very well.

Go to pages 34–35 for activities.

7 Birds

An Australian King Parrot

Some rainforest birds are very colorful. The Australian king parrot has a red head, green wings, and a blue tail. It has a yellow circle around each eye.

Hoatzin Birds

Hoatzin birds are black, brown, gray, orange, red, and blue. They live in the Amazon rainforest. Their babies have two claws on each wing. They use these claws to climb before they can fly.

Some rainforest birds are big. The female northern cassowary from Papua New Guinea can be up to 2 meters tall. It can weigh 58 kilograms. It has very big feet and it can't fly.

A Northern Cassowary

Other rainforest birds are very small. The smallest birds are hummingbirds. They drink nectar from flowers. They can flap their wings very fast – from 15 to 80 times every second.

A Hummingbird

Go to pages 36–37 for activities.

8 People

Many different groups of people live in tropical rainforests. The Penan people live in Sarawak. Sarawak is in Borneo in Asia. The Penan people travel through the rainforest in families of up to 30 people. Each family has one hut to live in and one smaller hut to sleep in. When they travel, they build new huts.

Building a Hut

Making Sago Flour

A Blowpipe

The Penan people make flour from sago palm trees. They hunt and eat deer, smaller mammals, and birds. Sometimes they use blowpipes to hunt.

The rainforest is the home of the Penan people, but some other people cut down the trees. Then the rainforest is different. Sometimes the Penan people can't find the plants that they use for medicines. Sometimes they can't find clean water or food.

Go to pages 38–39 for activities.

Rainforest Problems

Tropical rainforests are getting smaller. People cut down the trees to get wood. Then they sell the wood. Lots of furniture, doors, and floors are made from the wood.

Some farmers also cut down rainforest trees. They do this to keep cows on the land, or to grow coffee or sugar. Then they can sell the cows, coffee, and sugar.

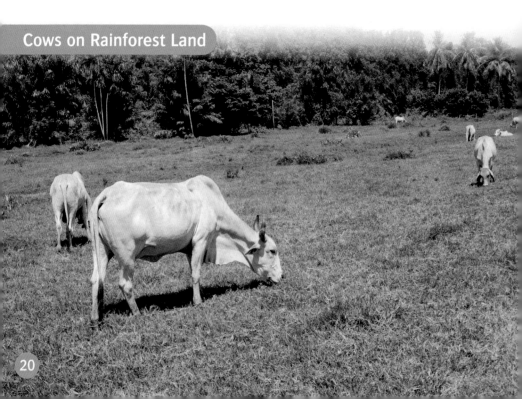

Cows on Rainforest Land

Trees are good for the soil. When there are no trees, the soil is not very good. Then new trees grow more slowly, and some trees die. With no trees, rainforest people and animals have no homes. They can't find food, and they can't live in the rainforest.

Discover!

People cut down about 20,000 square kilometers of rainforest every year. This is called deforestation.

→ Go to pages 40–41 for activities.

Save the Rainforests!

How can we save the tropical rainforests? We can buy coffee, sugar, and bananas from farmers who do not cut down rainforest trees. We can buy furniture that is not made from rainforest wood. We can buy recycled paper. This saves trees because paper is also made from wood.

A Sumatran Tiger

Discover!

Sumatran tigers live on the island of Sumatra in Indonesia in Asia. There are only about 250 tigers there. If we save rainforests, we can save tigers.

We can teach other people about rainforests and the people that live there. We can teach them about the amazing rainforest plants and rivers. We can teach them about the special mammals, birds, and minibeasts that live there, too.

Rainforests are beautiful and important places. Save the rainforests!

A Tree Frog

Go to pages 42–43 for activities.

1 Tropical Rainforests

← Read pages 4–5.

1 Write the numbers.

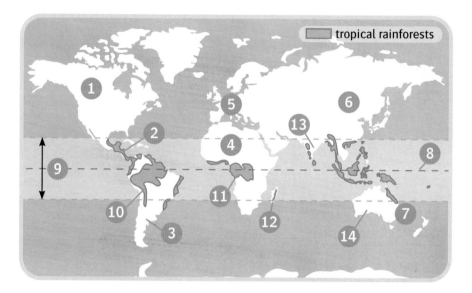

tropical rainforests

☐	Australasia	☐	Africa
☐	South America	☐	Asia
I	North America	☐	Europe
☐	Central America	☐	Equator
☐	The Tropics	☐	India
☐	Amazon rainforest	☐	Australia
☐	Congo rainforest	☐	Madagascar

2 Write ★ on your country. Circle the rainforest nearest to where you live.

3 Write the numbers.

50   400   6   750   1,500   150

1 Tropical rainforests cover only about __6__ % of Earth.

2 About _____ % of all the types of animal and plant live there.

3 About 10 square kilometers of rainforest can have _____ types of tree, _____ types of other plant, _____ types of bird, and _____ types of butterfly.

4 Answer the questions.

1 Where are all the tropical rainforests?

All the tropical rainforests are near the equator.

2 Where are most of the rainforests?

_____

3 Which is the biggest rainforest?

_____

4 Which is the second biggest rainforest?

_____

5 Where are the smaller rainforests?

_____

(2) Rainforest Layers

← Read pages 6–7.

forest floor   canopy
~~emergent layer~~   understory

1 **Write the words.**

1   _emergent layer_
2   _____
3   _____
4   _____

2 **Write the correct rainforest layer.**

1 It's dark and hot in the _understory_.

2 It's very windy in the _____.

3 There's light and lots of food in the _____.

4 The bottom layer is the _____.

5 The roots of the trees are on the _____.

6 The tops of the tallest trees are in the

_____.

7 The tops of the small trees are in the _____.

8 The big branches of the tall trees are in the

_____.

3 **Complete the chart.**

monkeys   ~~eagles~~   anteaters   bats
tree frogs   jaguars   insects   toucans

Emergent Layer	Canopy	Understory	Forest Floor
eagles	_____	_____	_____
_____	_____	_____	_____

4 **Look at the chart. Write sentences.**

1 ___Eagles___ and _____ live in the

emergent layer .

2 _____

3 _____

4 _____

③ Plants

← Read pages 8–9.

1 Write the words.

tanlp

lavees

chensrab

1   plant   2 _____   3 _____

tens

reet leho

4 _____   5 _____

2 Write *true* or *false*.

1 Plants are homes for rainforest animals.   true

2 Some small animals live in tree holes.   _____

3 Some birds make nests in tree holes.   _____

4 Orang-utans sleep in tree holes.   _____

5 Orang-utans make nests from bananas.   _____

6 Orang-utans sleep on the forest floor.   _____

3 What can we get or make from rainforest plants?

1 banana tree   →   b a n a n a s

2 balsa tree   →   w _ _ _

3 rubber tree   →   l _ _ _ _ _

4 nut tree   →   n _ _ _

5 pineapple leaves →   c _ _ _ _ _ _ _ and b _ _ _

4 Complete the sentences.

> grow   get   can   use   sleep   gives   ~~are~~   make

1 Many plants __are__ homes for rainforest animals.

2 Bananas, pineapples, and nuts _____ in the rainforest.

3 We _____ make things from rainforest plants.

4 We _____ some plants to make medicines.

5 The balsa tree _____ us wood.

6 We can _____ rubber with latex.

7 Animals and people _____ food from rainforest plants.

8 Some frogs _____ between the leaves of plants.

4 Rivers

left arrow Read pages 10–11.

1 Complete the puzzle.

1 a fish with big teeth
2 one of the biggest snakes in the world
3 a big river in Africa
4 a big river in Asia
5 the biggest rainforest river

Down 1:
p
i
r
a
n
h
a

2 →
3 ↓
4 →
5 →

2 Write ✓ or ✗.

1 The Mekong River is

[✗] bigger than the Amazon.

[✓] in Asia.

2 The Amazon isn't

[ ] a small river.

[ ] the biggest rainforest river.

3 The Amazon has more than 3,000

[ ] types of fish.

[ ] smaller rivers.

4 An anaconda is

[ ] a snake.

[ ] a fish.

5 Rivers give people

[ ] food and light.

[ ] food and water.

6 Many rainforest people travel by

[ ] train.

[ ] boat.

3 Write the words in the correct order.

1 live / rivers. / animals / Many / rainforest / in

Many animals live in rainforest rivers.

2 water. / give / Rivers / people

_____

3 Rivers / people /eat. / give / to / fish

_____

4 important / for / travel. / Rivers / are

_____

5 travel / on / boat / People / rivers. / by

_____

6 Amazon. / roads / aren't / There / many / the / in

_____

4 Write about the River Amazon.

The River Amazon is in _____

It's the _____

It's about _____

It has _____

_____ live in the River Amazon.

People need the river because _____

_____

← Read pages 12–13.

1 Find and write the words.

c	h	i	m	p	a	n	z	e	e
r	i	n	s	e	c	t	s	w	f
i	r	m	e	t	r	u	d	o	i
m	s	l	a	t	i	g	e	r	s
p	l	a	t	y	p	u	s	m	h
o	o	s	e	y	r	m	t	r	e
t	t	c	a	n	e	o	e	i	f
s	h	e	l	l	f	i	s	h	e

 1 ___fish___

 2 _____

 3 _____

 4 _____

5 _____

 6 _____

 7 _____

 8 _____

2 Circle the correct words.

1 The slowest mammals are **platypuses** / **sloths.**

2 The biggest cats in the world are **tigers** / **jaguars**.

3 Male **platypuses** / **tigers** have poisonous stingers.

4 **Chimpanzees** / **Tigers** live in African rainforests and eat leaves, fruit, and insects.

3 Complete the chart.

Mammals	Rainforest	Food
Chimpanzees	African rainforest	
Sloths		
Tigers		other mammals, fish, birds
Platypuses		

4 Draw and write about a rainforest mammal.

This is a _____

It lives _____

It eats _____

It _____

_____

_____

6 Minibeasts

← Read pages 14–15.

1 Use the code to write the animals. Then write the numbers.

a	b	d	e	f	h	i	l	m	n	o	p	r	s	t	u	y
⇩	⊙	✿	⋏	★	➚	▪	◆	⊕	❖	⊠	⬤	○	✿	⇧	☐	〰

1
⊙	☐	⇧	⇧	⋏	○	★	◆	〰
b	u	t	t	e	r	f	l	y

☐

2
⊕	⇩	❖	⇧	▪	✿

1

3
⊙	⋏	⋏	⇧	◆	⋏

☐

4
✿	⬤	▪	✿	⋏	○

☐

5
○	➚	▪	❖	⊠

☐

2 Match.

The female Queen Alexandra's Birdwing	are probably the biggest spiders.
Rhinoceros beetles	can look like flowers.
Tarantulas	is the biggest butterfly.
Mantises	have horns like rhinos.

3 Correct the sentences.

1 The Queen Alexandra's Birdwing lives in India.

   The Queen Alexandra's Birdwing lives in Papua New Guinea.

2 Most of the minibeasts in rainforests are spiders.

   _____

3 Mantises can't use camouflage.

   _____

4 Rhinoceros beetles have a stinger on their head.

   _____

5 Tarantulas live in African rainforests.

   _____

6 Tarantulas have six eyes.

   _____

7 Birds

← Read pages 16–17.

1 Write the words.

> tail   wing   feet   eye   head

1 _____

2 _____

3 _____

4 _____

5 _____

2 Circle the correct words.

1 The Australian king parrot is **colorful** / **black and white**.

2 Hoatzin **babies** / **adults** climb before they can fly.

3 Hoatzin babies have claws on their **head** / **wings**.

4 The female northern cassowary can weigh **58** / **85** kilograms.

5 The northern cassowary **can** / **can't** fly.

6 Hummingbirds flap their wings very **fast** / **slowly**.

3 Complete the chart.

> It has very big feet   It flaps its wings very fast.
> ~~It has a yellow circle around each eye.~~
> It can be 2 meters tall.   Its babies can climb.
> It's very small.   It lives in the Amazon.
> It's red, blue, green, and yellow.

Australian King Parrot	It has a yellow circle around each eye.
Hoatzin	
Female Northern Cassowary	
Hummingbird	

4 Write about two rainforest birds.

Name: _____

_____

_____

Name: _____

_____

_____

8 People

← Read pages 18–19.

1 Complete the puzzle. Write the secret word.

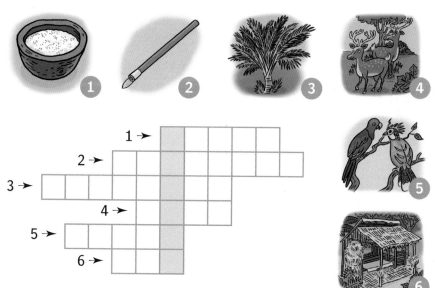

The secret word is: ⬜⬜⬜⬜⬜⬜

2 Complete the sentences with words from activity 1.

1 The Penan people hunt _____ and _____.

2 They have a _____ to sleep in.

3 They make and eat sago _____.

4 They make flour from the sago _____.

5 They sometimes use a _____ to hunt.

3 Answer the questions.

1 Where do the Penan people live?

_____

2 How many huts does each family have?

_____

3 What do they eat?

_____

4 Why can't the Penan people find the trees that they need?

_____

4 Draw and write about the Penan people.

The Penan people are rainforest people from

_____

_____

_____

_____

_____

← Read pages 20–21.

1 Find and write the words.

owoododfloorrunfurnitureeddooringcoworcoffeesosugar

1 wood   2 _____   3 _____   4 _____

5 _____   6 _____   7 _____

2 Number the sentences in order.

☐ They sell the wood.

☐ Other people make furniture, doors, and floors.

☐ People cut down rainforest trees.

☐ They get wood from the trees.

3 Match.

1 Some farmers cut down
2 They keep
3 Some farmers grow
4 Then they sell

cows on the land.

rainforest trees.

the cows, coffee, and sugar.

coffee or sugar.

4 Complete the diagram.

slowly ~~soil~~ homes die live food

When people cut down trees ...

1 The __soil__ is not very good.

2 New trees grow more _____ .

3 Some trees _____ .

4 Rainforest people and animals have no _____ .

5 Rainforest people and animals can't find _____ to eat.

6 Rainforest people and animals can't _____ in the rainforest.

10 Save the Rainforests!

← Read pages 22–23.

1 Write the words in order. Then write ✓ or ✗.

1 trees. / down / Cut / rainforest

   Cut down rainforest trees. _____ ✗

2 wood. / furniture / from / rainforest / Buy / made

   _____ ☐

3 rainforests. / people / Teach / about

   _____ ☐

4 paper. / recycled / Buy

   _____ ☐

5 down / farmers / who / coffee / from / Buy / trees. / cut / rainforest

   _____

   _____ ☐

2 Complete the words.

We can teach people about rainforest ...

1 p _ _ _ _ _   4 m _ _ _ _ _ _

2 p _ _ _ _ _   5 b _ _ _ _

3 r _ _ _ _ _   6 m _ _ _ _ _ _ _ _ _

3 Complete the sentences.

Indonesia tigers rainforests Sumatra

1 Sumatran tigers live on the island of _____ .

2 Sumatra is in _____ .

3 There are only about 250 Sumatran _____ on Sumatra.

4 If we save _____ , we can save tigers.

4 Which tropical rainforest is it?

1 It's the biggest tropical rainforest. _____

2 It's the second biggest tropical rainforest. _____

3 It has the biggest rainforest river. _____

4 The Mekong River is here. _____

5 Platypuses live here. _____

6 Tigers live here. _____

7 Chimpanzees live here. _____

8 Tarantulas live here. _____

9 Hoatzin birds live here. _____

10 The Penan people live here. _____

A Tropical Rainforest

1 Draw a map of the tropical rainforest nearest where you live.

2 Draw the rainforest rivers on your map. Write the names of the rivers.

3 Draw and write about a mammal, a bird, and a minibeast from this rainforest.

_____

_____

_____

_____

_____

_____

_____

_____

_____

Save the Rainforests!

1 How can we save the rainforests? Write notes.

When people cut down trees ...

New trees _____

Some trees _____

_____

_____

How can we save the rainforests?

We can teach _____

We can save _____

We can buy _____

We can _____

_____

2 Make a poster about how to save the rainforests.

3 Display your poster.

Picture Dictionary

 breathe

 buy

 chimpanzee

 claws

 climb

 clothes

 coffee

 dark

 deer

 die

 female

 food

 forest

 fruit

 furniture

 grow

 hide

 hole

 hunt

 insects

island

 land

 male

 medicines

 percent (%)

 pineapple

 plants

 poisonous

 recycle

 rhino

 river

 road

 rubber

 shellfish

 soil

 square kilometer

 stick

 sugar

 wood

 worm

47

Oxford Read and Discover

Series Editor: Hazel Geatches • CLIL Adviser: John Clegg

Oxford Read and Discover graded readers are at six levels, for students from age 6 and older. They cover many topics within three subject areas, and support English across the curriculum, or Content and Language Integrated Learning (CLIL).

Available for each reader:
• Audio Pack
• Activity Book

Available for selected readers:
• e-Books

Teaching notes & CLIL guidance: www.oup.com/elt/teacher/readanddiscover

Subject Area / Level	The World of Science & Technology	The Natural World	The World of Arts & Social Studies
1 300 headwords	• Eyes • Fruit • Trees • Wheels	• At the Beach • In the Sky • Wild Cats • Young Animals	• Art • Schools
2 450 headwords	• Electricity • Plastic • Sunny and Rainy • Your Body	• Camouflage • Earth • Farms • In the Mountains	• Cities • Jobs
3 600 headwords	• How We Make Products • Sound and Music • Super Structures • Your Five Senses	• Amazing Minibeasts • Animals in the Air • Life in Rainforests • Wonderful Water	• Festivals Around the World • Free Time Around the World
4 750 headwords	• All About Plants • How to Stay Healthy • Machines Then and Now • Why We Recycle	• All About Desert Life • All About Ocean Life • Animals at Night • Incredible Earth	• Animals in Art • Wonders of the Past
5 900 headwords	• Materials to Products • Medicine Then and Now • Transportation Then and Now • Wild Weather	• All About Islands • Animal Life Cycles • Exploring Our World • Great Migrations	• Homes Around the World • Our World in Art
6 1,050 headwords	• Cells and Microbes • Clothes Then and Now • Incredible Energy • Your Amazing Body	• All About Space • Caring for Our Planet • Earth Then and Now • Wonderful Ecosystems	• Food Around the World • Helping Around the World